THE VANISHING DEPOT

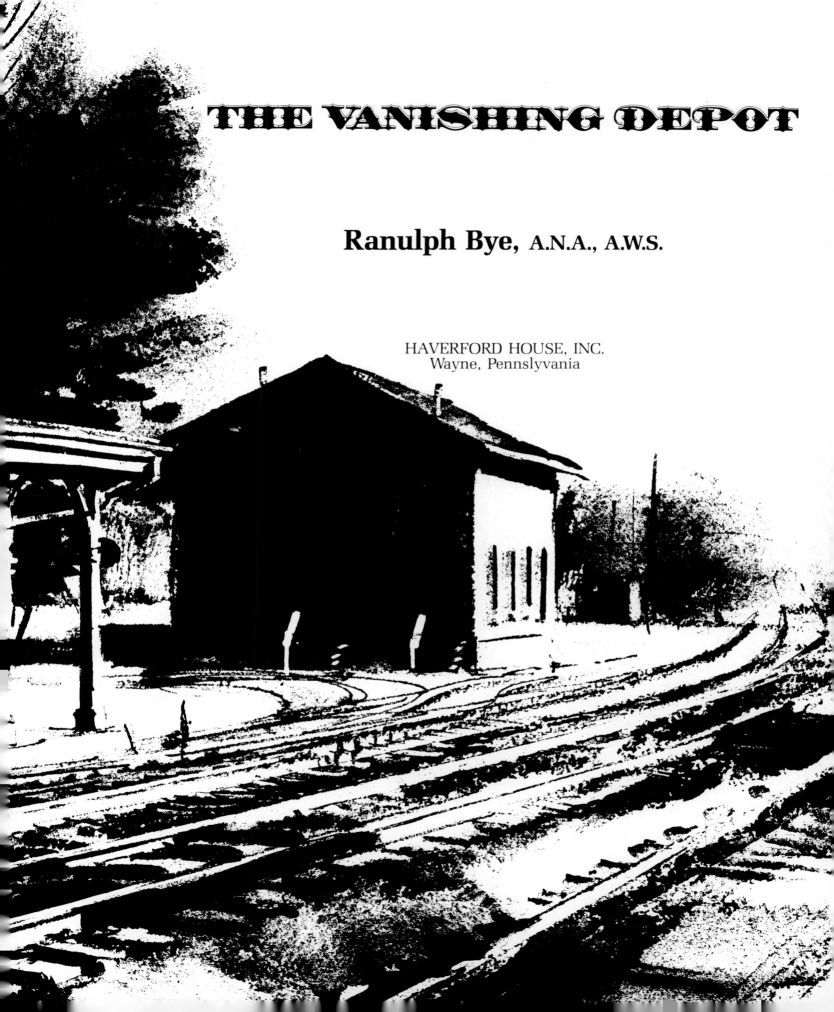

THE VANISHING DEPOT

Ranulph Bye, A.N.A., A.W.S.

HAVERFORD HOUSE, INC.
Wayne, Pennslyvania

HAVERFORD HOUSE, INC.
34 West Avenue
Box 408
Wayne, PA 19087
U.S.A.

Revised and reprinted by Haverford House, Inc. 1983
Copyright © 1983 by Ranulph Bye

Library of Congress Cataloging in Publication Data

Bye, Ranulph, 1916—
  The vanishing depot.

  1. Bye, Ranulph, 1916— 2. Railroads—United
States—Stations—Pictorial works. I. Title.
Library of Congress Catalog Card No. 83-082455
ISBN 0-910702-11-X

FOR

GLENNA   CATHERINE

Contents

Where is the bustle and chatter
  The sound of the clanging gates?
The clock that a gentleman hurries
  As a loved one he awaits?

Where are the redcaps and porters,
  The engineer, King of the Day?
Like a mist falling over the ocean
  Their image is fading away.

This depot was once lord of Main Street
  The Victorian master of town
Now the windows and shutters are broken
  Its torn roof is sagging down.

What wonderful memories it harbors
  The echoes of laughter and tears
Like a scene from the past in a daydream
  The depot disappears.

Rita Loftus Gross

Foreword

In the early days of railroading, the local depot was a source of community pride. As time passed, it generally was taken for granted, a hardly-noticed town fixture. Only recently has it, once again, come into focus, since the curtailment of passenger services has signalled the end of many a landmark.

Railroadiana always had many enthusiasts, because of the historical importance of locomotives and rolling stock. With the cutback in passenger service, many more have joined the ranks of railroad buffs, looking back with nostalgia at this significant part of Americana.

The sudden boom in railroad interest carried over to the stations. In this volume, Mr. Bye's talents help perpetuate these structures for us, and rekindle memories of railroading in its heyday. He has painted these buildings of that bygone era and given each a lasting measure of pride. I know that as you look at each painting, you will agree.

EDWIN P. ALEXANDER

Preface

This book is an attempt to illustrate some of the unique stations I have come across in my travels up and down the east coast during the past 12 years. All the stations depicted here in watercolor were painted on location or from pictures taken on the spot. It is regrettable that many have been razed since this project began. Since most of the more interesting stations were built during the early days of railroading over a century ago, I am limiting this study to depots built prior to 1900 except, in rare cases, where I found a few of particular interest built since that period. Included here are also freight stations, signal towers, watchman's shanties and some architectural details of stations. To keep the book in its historical context the identification of stations is related to the railroads which they originally served, and not necessarily the present operating company.

I express appreciation to the following institutions which have kindly given permission to have their works reproduced: The Smithsonian Institution (National Museum of History and Technology) and the William Penn Museum of the Pennsylvania Historical and Museum Commission in Harrisburg. Also to Edwin P. Alexander for making available his research material, and to the American Heritage Publishing Company for the information it provided.

Many people were kind enough to answer my letters of inquiry, return my phone calls, and volunteer to dig through records to help me research this book. George Hart of the Pennsylvania Historical and Museum Commission, W. C. Humphreys, and Al Chamberlain of Penn Central Railroad, Edgar A. Riddle of the Lehigh Valley Railroad, Harry P. Albrecht, Publisher *Steam Locomotives of Yesteryear,* James M. Bourne, of the Baltimore and Ohio Railroad, Lois Morasco, W. H. Kiehl, The Chessie System, Nathan James, and George W. Eastland are a few of these people, and to those others inadvertantly omitted, my sincere thanks.

I also wish to express my gratitude to my friend and colleague, Bill Loos, whose creative endeavor designed this book. And Mr. Kent Day Coes for his helpful assistance in updating the revised captions.

Introduction

This is a nostalgic journey into the golden age of railroading, the wondrous years that ended in the 1920's. The great iron horse was king of the road, well into its second century, but still full of steam and rarin' to go. But youthful contenders loomed large on the horizon, ready to take their places in transport history, the automobile, the airplane. Yet they, and no other means of transportation, ever achieved the personality of the old passenger train; and neither garage nor airport fell heir to the character and fascination of the rural depot.

Railroading had a resurgence or two after the 20's, serving our country well in the movement of men and material during the war years. But the trend which began in 1929 continued. Diminishing fares brought deficits to the lines with the consequent curtailment of passenger service and the demise of many country stations.

The depot was the hub of hamlet and town for 125 years. Not only was it the center of transportation, but the main source of communication and the symbol of the high road to adventure and opportunity. Lucius Beebe said that no other single structure or edifice has occupied as compelling a place in American consciousness as the railroad depot.

While Europe had already constructed magnificent terminals by 1865, the United States had mostly poorly-planned and makeshift buildings which were often constructed of wood that could be expected to go up in smoke at the first spark. By the 70's and 80's we were at least trying to compete, but the result was more often quaint, rather than magnificent. For the most part, the terminals reflected the individual architectural tastes of the wealthy owners of this booming industry.

In an attempt to imitate styles from abroad Americans were fond of using towers of some sort, preferably the picturesque features of Norman, Italian, Rhenish castle or some other unlikely design. Stations built from 1875 on were house-like structures incorporating all the architectural gimcracks of the period. The Queen Anne style was represented by a massive conical tower such as was used in Easton and Mauch Chunk (now Jim Thorpe, Pennsylvania). Sometimes a large cupola would set it apart from the ordinary. Most stations located in built-up areas had accommodations for the agents and their families who lived upstairs. The smaller depots on back country spurs were simple affairs containing only a waiting room and ticket office, and perhaps a separate room for baggage. They often resembled fancy gate houses of large estates found in the suburbs of big cities. The most distinguishing feature of the American depot was the copious overhanging roof which usually skirted the entire building to give protection for passengers on the platforms and entranceways. It is the hallmark of the "Railroad Style." As passenger service increased, even the platforms themselves were covered with a roof for 200 feet or more.

In New England, New Jersey, Pennsylvania and elsewhere, a gabled roof was simply extended in a straight line from the peak to 9 or 12 feet beyond the side of the building. In the case of two-story buildings, the overhang was supported by use of immense brackets. In stone or brick buildings these brackets were held in place by stone notches which extended a few inches from the outside wall.

The mansard roof was frequently used during the short era prior to 1876 and was commonly known as "General Grant Style", although this is a rather loose designation which took in everything with a mansard roof. Excellent examples of this style can be found in Bethlehem Pennsylvania, Hopewell and Pennington, New Jersey.

Throughout the 1850's, the railroads serving such cities as Philadelphia, New York, Harrisburg and Baltimore erected a number of substantial stations, and this trend became well established for years. Comparatively few smaller stations were architecturally designed. Generally most were planned by the railroads' engineering departments, built under their supervision by their carpenters and engineers. Stations by the hundreds, even thousands, were just utilitarian buildings. Fortunately, many others were distinctive in some form or other and these are the ones we remember for their picturesque quality.

Today the local railroad station is vanishing from the rural American scene almost as fast as the vanishing passenger train. And one can never be sure whether that one-story building standing forlornly where the depot used to be will house a lumber yard, office or a boutique.

The alert motorist who frequents the byways, rather than the turnpikes, can add to his touring enjoyment by making a game of searching out and identifying present and past railroad stations. This is not always easy, because the gables and scrollwork that were part of the late 19th-century architecture are rapidly disappearing behind advertising signs. In many cases all that is left is a bare spot on the ground where a station once stood, with only a broken cement platform left as a reminder. Stations on the Erie Lackawanna also are following the inevitable. For example, the building at Mountain Lakes, New Jersey is now a firehouse. Among the entries on the Delaware & Hudson's right of way are a firehouse, a shopping center and a discount store. And so it goes.

There are only a few stations still functioning today as they did during the heyday of American railroading, thanks to the resurgence of interest by railroad buffs. The New Hope, Pennsylvania depot is still in its original condition in spite of having been moved twice. Also in their original conditions are stations at Kempton and Strasburg, Pennsylvania, Middletown, New York, Hopewell, New Jersey and a beautiful one in Chester, Vermont.

Numbers of stations have been restored, such as the Fanwood, New Jersey and Bethlehem, Pennsylvania depots, by the Junior Chamber of Commerce, but these are no longer in service by the railroad. Suburban stations are still in use around metropolitan centers of the country for the convenience of commuters. But, for the most part, the rural station is now a memory of the past and the few that are left standing are boarded up or have been converted into a more profitable enterprise.

Says John Maas in *The Gingerbread Age:* "Today the railroad station is often a backwater on the wrong side of town. In the nineteenth century it was the hub of the community, the link to the Great World— the wretched roads were blocked by snow and mud for months, good highways came only after the automobile. Railroading was the nineteenth century's premier industry. It offered the finest careers to ambitious men, the most jobs to skilled workers. The Victorian railroad depot was a place of glamour and excitement and designed to look the part."

THE VANISHING DEPOT

Collection of John A. Meyer, Jr., Coach Inn, Ft. Washington, Pa.

ALLENTOWN, PENNSYLVANIA

As part of the Central Railroad of New Jersey, this brick building once served such noted trains as the Scranton Flyer, the Queen of the Valley and the Harrisburg Special. The station dates back to 1903 and is presently used as a restaurant.

ALLENTOWN, PENNSYLVANIA

The interlocking tower at the Union Street
Crossing was a box-like structure,
situated near the Auburn Street Crossing
tower. It was razed after the station it
served discontinued service.

21

Ranulph Bye

ALLENTOWN, PENNSYLVANIA

For more than 60 years the famous Black Diamond Express made Allentown a regular stop on its run. So did the Wyoming Valley Express, The Maple Leaf and The Star of the Buffalo-Toronto Express and the Lehigh Limited!

This monolithic structure, built in 1890, was on the main line of the Lehigh Valley Railroad between New York and Buffalo. Its foundation was unique in that it was actually built into the East Hamilton Street bridge that crossed over its tracks. The station, abandoned in 1962, was sold with its surrounding land, probably for land development.

Photo by Pennsylvania Historical and Museum Commission, Harrisburg, Pennsylvania

ALLENTOWN, PENNSYLVANIA

This elevated structure was the watchman's shelter and gate control house. It once was located near the signal tower at the Auburn Street crossing. It has since been demolished.

ALLENTOWN, PENNSYLVANIA

Actually more of an elevated watchman's
shanty than a signal tower, this structure
at the Auburn Street Crossing has been
demolished since the artist painted it.

Similar towers are fast disappearing
from the scene as the computer world,
the great mechanics of our age, replace
small watchman's shanties.

BIRDSBORO, PENNSYLVANIA

The Wilmington & Reading Division of
the Reading Company joins the main
stem of the Philadelphia & Reading at
Birdsboro.

    This frame structure, built about 1910,
has some unusual features, which include
a raised platform skirting the entire
building and a graceful arch spanning
the inside gable. The depot appeared to
be unused when painted by the artist on
April 16, 1973.

BETHLEHEM, PENNSYLVANIA

The architectural style of the 1850's coupled with the French influence which produced the mansard roof, was highly acclaimed and enthusiastically received. The overhanging roof offered protection to passengers on the platform. Because it was supported by large brackets, it needed no pillars, and thus did not interfere with passengers boarding the train.

The station was built in 1873, and was once part of the Central Railroad of New Jersey. It served the most luxurious trains running from New York to Harrisburg.

Since 1966 the Junior Chamber of Commerce has demonstrated its interest in this remarkable structure by restoring the exterior and completely modernizing the interior. The station now serves as a restaurant.

Photo by Pennsylvania Historical and Museum Commission. Harrisburg, Pennsylvania

Collection of Division of Mechanical & Civil Engineering Museum of History and Technology, Smithsonian Institution

BLOOMSBURG, PENNSYLVANIA

Built in 1908, the watchman's shanty at
Bloomsburg is an example of the kind of
tiny building that was once common
throughout this country. It gave warmth
and cover to the crossing attendant in
inclement weather.

It was sold in 1966 and is now part of
a railroad museum.

EASTON, PENNSYLVANIA

This comparatively recent structure, built
in 1927 is typical of most signal towers
with its concrete foundation and brick
walls, and is topped by an
asbestos-shingled wooden roof.

Photo by Pennsylvania Historical and Museum Commission, Harrisburg, Pennsylvania

EASTON, PENNSYLVANIA

The town of Easton, at the junction of the Lehigh and Delaware Rivers, has been a center of transportation since colonial times.

The present station was constructed in 1887 on a railroad line opened in 1867; it is not the original building. At one time the Easton station, on the main line between New York and Harrisburg, served the finest trains operating between New York and Chicago.

The stations at Easton, Bethlehem, Allentown, and Jim Thorpe were all painted by the artist when they were part of the Central Railroad of New Jersey, prior to their being acquired by the Lehigh Valley Railroad System in 1971. Station burned down in mid 70's.

31

Ranulph Bye

GETTYSBURG, PENNSYLVANIA

In 1863 President Lincoln arrived by train to deliver his famous address. It was also the home station for President Eisenhower, the most distinguished resident of Gettysburg. Through the years it served a number of official trains, as well as many visitors to this historic site.

This is a beautiful station with an elegant cupola; still the original building on the original site. The station was built by the Gettysburg Railroad in 1858 on the old Hanover Junction and Gettysburg Line. It later became part of the Western Maryland Railroad system.

During the Civil War it was an important depot for evacuating the wounded from the battlefield. Today the station has been converted to the home of the Gettysburg Tourist Bureau.

JIM THORPE, PENNSYLVANIA

The town of Jim Thorpe, formerly known as Mauch Chunk, and renamed to honor the legendary Indian athlete, is located about 40 miles south of Wilkes-Barre. Its brick, two-story station with steeple-type roof is a counterpart of the one at Easton. The depot was built in 1888 and at one time accommodated literally hundreds of excursion trains in a season.

It was also the commercial outlet of anthracite to Philadelphia and New York markets, and the home of millionaires associated with the flourishing coal industry.

Jim Thorpe had two stations; this is the only one still extant and it has been remodeled into business offices and visitors center.

LEBANON, PENNSYLVANIA

Lebanon Station was designed in 1885 by
Philadelphia architect, George W. Hewitt
for the iron-ore baron, Robert Coleman.
The Cornwall-Lebanon Railroad as it was
known was a short line railroad consisting
of 22 miles of track extending to
Conewago on the Pennsylvania Railroad
mainline. Primarily, the building was a
train station; however, during World War
II it functioned as a bus depot and more
recently housed a dress factory.

Photo by Pennsylvania Historical and Museum Commission, Harrisburg, Pennsylvania

NORTHUMBERLAND, PENNSYLVANIA

The brick station at Northumberland is located in scenic Montour County, on the point formed by the confluence of the north and west branches of the Susquehanna River, approximately 55 miles north of Harrisburg.

This is the original building; the present station was built in 1910 and has recently been converted to another use.

Ranulph Bye

REINHOLDS, PENNSYLVANIA

Reinholds station was built in 1905 in the
heart of the Pennsylvania Dutch country,
13 miles west of Reading, and was on the
Lancaster branch of the Reading Railroad.
It is now being used by a commercial
plumbing and heating company. The
Reinholds Hotel is also pictured.

SCRANTON FREIGHT STATION
SCRANTON, PENNSYLVANIA
Central Railroad of New Jersey
West Lackawanna Ave., Scranton
Wilson Brothers, Philadelphia
architects-contractors, 1891

The Scranton Freight Station has played a
key role in the fortunes of Scranton.
During the ascendancy of coal, from 1866
to 1919, this fuel was shipped through
Scranton to Philadelphia and the rest of
the nation. The town, in the heart of
Pennsylvania's Wyoming Valley, handled
coal from Carbondale in the north to
Nanticoke in the south. In 1891, during
these boom days, the Central Railroad of
New Jersey built Scranton Freight Station.
The building combines the Queen Anne

and Richardsonian Romanesque styles.
   As with countless fine old buildings,
parts of the station are in advanced decay.
The Wilson Brothers of Philadelphia, were
the most important railroad station
architects of the railway boom days. The
company was responsible for stations from
Vermont to Colorado, including such
terminals as the Reading in Philadelphia,
and the first Broad Street Station in the
same city, now demolished.

Ramulph Bye

SINKING SPRING, PENNSYLVANIA

The Lebanon Valley branch of the Reading
Company once served this station. Its
one-story, irregularly-shaped frame
building with freight house dates back to
1872. The railroad line opened in 1859.
The station has been demolished.

TOPTON, PENNSYLVANIA

Situated in a small town, 19 miles east of
Reading, the Topton depot is a one-story
brick structure.

The depot, now on the Reading line,
was completed in 1874 for the North
Pennsylvania Railroad, which began
operations in 1869.

Collection of John A. Meyer, Jr., Coach Inn, Ft. Washington, Pa.

WILKES-BARRE, PENNSYLVANIA

This Wilkes-Barre depot was built in 1870 as part of the Lehigh Valley Railroad System. It had two stories, but the main feature was its irregularly-shaped brick construction. It was sold with its surrounding land in 1963 and was later demolished.

WILKES-BARRE, PENNSYLVANIA
William George Burns, architect

Patterned, perhaps, after a Victorian dovecote and built in 1868, this many gabled structure boasts walls of brick a foot thick. Located on East Market Street, it was built to replace the former station near River Common, and was considered a model of its time. It was part of the Central Railroad of New Jersey on the main line between Scranton and Jersey City. Passenger service was discontinued in 1963 but in the mid 70's the station was completely remodeled into a restaurant with parlor cars attached to the old depot.

YORK, PENNSYLVANIA

York station was built sometime between 1885 and 1895 as part of the Northern Central Railway Company. It was later leased by Penn Central.

It was on a line between Washington and Harrisburg. It is still associated with the old depot hotel across the street, which is still standing. Since April of 1973 the station itself is not in service as such.

ELLICOTT CITY, MARYLAND

This depot is another real old timer, built in 1831, unusually well-preserved despite its age. It was declared a National Historic Landmark in 1968.

Ellicott City prospered for awhile after the station was built, but went downhill. The town was rejuvenated when the Tom Thumb, a tiny woodburning "vertical boiler", made its historic maiden voyage on the nation's first railroad track, which was part of the Baltimore & Ohio Railroad. The route of the Tom Thumb was from Baltimore to Ellicott's Mill, approximately 13 miles away.

This gives the impression that the town was rejuvenated by the Tom Thumb. The latter ran a race with a horse—and lost!

GAITHERSBURG, MARYLAND

Gaithersburg has a charming station which dates back to 1878. Of particular interest is the use of spools and spindles under the overhang, rather an unusual trim.

It is on the Baltimore & Ohio's main line and the next station after Rockville to Point of Rocks, Harpers Ferry and Cumberland; it is between Cumberland and Washington, D.C.

The station, with ticket office, is still used by commuters.

LAUREL, MARYLAND

On the main line of the Baltimore & Ohio Railroad, Laurel is about halfway between Baltimore and Washington. The station was built in 1903. Pittsburgh, Chicago and St. Louis trains used the tracks until 1957.

45

POINT OF ROCKS, MARYLAND

Designed by architect E. Francis Baldwin
and built in 1875. The present two-story
brick station at Point of Rocks, complete
with Italianate stonework and Bavarian
bell tower, still stands as a fine example of
Neo-Gothic design.

There was a predecessor at this site,
opened by the Baltimore & Ohio line in
the early 1830's.

ROCKVILLE, MARYLAND

This attractive two-story brick station at Rockville is of Gothic design and dates back to 1878. On the Baltimore & Ohio's main line, the depot is approximately 12 miles northwest of Washington, D.C.

TAKOMA PARK, MARYLAND

Takoma Park, just north of our nation's
capitol, once was served by this station,
a stop on the Baltimore & Ohio line.
Built in 1893, the single-story frame
structure fell victim to fire a few years
ago.

CLAYTON, DELAWARE

It must have been an exciting time for Clayton when, in 1884, the Philadelphia & Norfolk Railroad completed tracks for its Delaware Division (later incorporated into the Pennsylvania System).

This colorful station, with its semicircular fanlight over the windows and doorway, was ready to welcome passengers. Clayton is about 37 miles south of Wilmington.

GRAFTON, WEST VIRGINIA

Located on the Tygate Valley River. In
1857 excavations were made for hotel and
station for the Baltimore & Ohio Railroad,
formerly the North West Virginia Railroad.
Date on present hotel: John T. McGraw
1911. Date of station circa 1910-12.

Collection of John A. Meyer, Jr., Coach Inn, Ft. Washington, Pa.

HARPERS FERRY, WEST VIRGINIA

This historic town, 55 miles northwest of Washington, D.C., takes pride in its two-story station, built in 1894.

Harpers Ferry was established as a U.S. arsenal in 1796; it is famous as the site of John Brown's raid in 1859, which signaled the start of the Civil War. In the war between the states, Harpers Ferry was of strategic importance, situated as it was at the lower end of the Shenandoah Valley. The occupation of the arsenal changed from Federal to Confederate hands a number of times as the war progressed. After the battle of Gettysburg, it remained in Federal hands until the cessation of hostilities in 1865.

The depot is now a National Parks Service Historic Site.

OVERBROOK, PHILADELPHIA, PENNSYLVANIA

This frame building has a large over-hanging roof to protect passengers on the platform. The station itself consists of a waiting room and ticket office; living quarters are attached.

Overbrook was a country station until 1890. It dates back to the 1870's and served a railroad line that had opened in 1849. It once had a proud bearing, but has been neglected of late.

The station is situated on the Philadelphia-Montgomery County boundary line, near City Line Avenue.

52

Ranulph Bye

BRYN MAWR, PENNSYLVANIA

Located on the main line of the Penn
Central, 10 miles from Broad Street
Station, this freight house was completed
sometime in the 1870's. It's roof has a
chopped gable, a type known as "jerkin'
head."

There was an adjacent depot but it was
torn down to make way for a small
utilitarian structure.

Photo by Pennsylvania Historical and Museum Commission, Harrisburg, Pennsylvania

WAYNE, PENNSYLVANIA

Typical of present suburban stations
between Paoli and 30th Street Station,
Wayne is a Penn Central stop on the
commuter route to Philadelphia.

In the old days, between 1833 and
1857, the depot was on the Main Line
of Public Works, Philadelphia to
Pittsburgh. The Main Line of Public Works
was a system of railways and canals
linking Philadelphia with the Ohio River
ordered by the Pennsylvania Legislative
in 1828.

Ralph Bye

STRAFFORD, PENNSYLVANIA

This building was one of the attractions at the Philadelphia Centennial and was built in Japan for use as that country's contribution to the Exposition. After the exposition was over, the station was moved to its present site on the Penn Central's Main Line and has been in continual use since 1887.

The depot has lost none of its unique charm and is very well maintained, still used by commuters.

COSSART STATION, PENNSYLVANIA

Originally Cossart Station was an old dwelling built in 1895. Complete with a porch, this frame structure always looked more like a farmhouse than a depot.

Cossart Station is located in the Brandywine Valley, 13 miles north of Wilmington, Delaware. It was at one time on the Wilmington & Northern Railroad and was later leased to the Reading Railroad.

A two-story stone station and agents dwelling was built in 1929 to replace the frame depot. This stone structure now serves as an office and storage area for a farm.

Ranulph Bye

DOYLESTOWN, PENNSYLVANIA

The first major outlet to the great outside world was in 1856, when a branch of the North Pennsylvania Railroad began service, uniting with the main line at Lansdale, 10 miles away. Until then, the stage coach was the link between Doylestown and Philadelphia.

This substantial station, built in 1871, was operated by The Reading Company.

Collection of Division of Mechanical & Civil Engineering Museum of History and Technology, Smithsonian Institution

FAIRMOUNT PARK, PHILADELPHIA, PENNSYLVANIA

On the Reading line, the quaint signal
tower was dwarfed when the Expressway,
towering overhead, was opened to traffic.
It was dismantled in 1966.

GLEN MILLS, PENNSYLVANIA

Another from the 1880's, this station was part of the Philadelphia & Baltimore, later served by the Pennsylvania Railroad. Constructed of brick, it has the fairly common two stories, with ticket office and living quarters.

It's situated about 20 miles southwest of Philadelphia.

WISSAHICKON, PHILADELPHIA, PENNSYLVANIA

This freight station was built in 1892 on the Philadelphia-Reading Railroad, a line which opened in 1836. The passenger station appearing in the background is on its original site as well.

60

Ranulph Bye

MT. AIRY, PHILADELPHIA,
PENNSYLVANIA

This two-story frame passenger station
was completed in 1883 for the former
Philadelphia & Reading Railway. It cost
approximately $8,000.
 On the Chestnut Hill branch of the
Reading, the station is a little over 9
miles from the company's terminal in
Philadelphia.

ALLEN LANE, PHILADELPHIA, PENNSYLVANIA

Although the station itself is not represented in this view, the lower level platform, protective walkways and overpass are shown.

Built in 1884, the depot is on the Chestnut Hill Branch of the Penn Central, formerly the Pennsylvania Railroad. Its design is typical of most on this line; waiting room and ticket office downstairs, living quarters above.

UPSAL, PHILADELPHIA
PENNSYLVANIA

The depot is partially of brick, designed in the Victorian style known as "Gingerbread." The Pennsylvania Railroad opened its Chestnut Hill line to rival that of the Reading in 1884, and this station probably dates from that period. It is quite similar to the station at Strafford, but not as old.

GRAVERS STATION
CHESTNUT HILL, PHILADELPHIA

This exclusive suburban area was first directly connected with the city in 1854 when the Chestnut Hill Railroad was opened. Leased together with the Philadelphia, Germantown & Norristown Railroad by the Reading in 1870, the line was spruced up with extremely handsome stations. Frank Furness was Philadelphia's most noted Victorian architect and Gravers (also known as Gravers Lane), built in 1883, was one of the most successful designs for the Reading. The building is now rented.

Collection of Eugene Maginnis

CHESTNUT HILL, PHILADELPHIA, PENNSYLVANIA 1884

To live in the suburbs is an old Philadelphia tradition. To breath fresh air and relax, affluent merchants and politicians escaped—at least for the summer—to the healthful higher reaches. Upper and lower Germantown, and to a lesser extent, Chestnut Hill, became meccas of suburban life.

Among the first railroads to be built was the Philadelphia, Germantown and Norristown in the 1830's. By 1884 the Pennsylvania opened a branch line to Chestnut Hill which is illustrated as it looks today. The station still serves commuters and trains still run regularly.

COLLEGEVILLE DEPOT, MONTGOMERY
COUNTY, PENNSYLVANIA

Property of the Reading Company, where
trains once stopped often, is now
out-of-service.

PERKASIE, PENNSYLVANIA

Another one-story freight station representative of most of its time. Freight handling began in 1887.

The passenger station, which came four years later, can be seen in the background. Both facilities are still in existence, but only the freight office is operating.

Ranulph Bye

SELLERSVILLE, PENNSYLVANIA

Initially this was Sellers Tavern on the
Bethlehem Pike. The irregularly-shaped
brick structure, built in 1901, was
converted into a passenger station by the
North Pennsylvania Railroad, which had
been operating since 1857.

SOUTHHAMPTON, PENNSYLVANIA

Depot and freight station on the Newtown
branch of the Reading Railroad.

NEW BRITAIN, PENNSYLVANIA

Another diamond jubilee model, typical
of the country depots built just before
the turn of the century . . . frame
construction, single-story, with a peak
roof. It has an agent's office and waiting
room; the freight house is separate. It is
served by the Doylestown Branch of the
Reading Company, and is roughly 32
miles north of Philadelphia. Station
burned down a few years ago.

NORTH WALES, PENNSYLVANIA

The distinguishing feature of this station is the use of iron supports under the overhanging roof instead of wooden beams. The iron supports evidently were experimental, since this method was not used on later and similar stations.

Built in 1860 on a railroad line opened four years prior, the North Wales station was leased to the Reading Company in 1879. North Wales is 22 miles from Philadelphia on the main line to Bethlehem, Pennsylvania. The station is in active use.

Collection of Mr. and Mrs. Wm. J. Gross

NEW HOPE, PENNSYLVANIA

New Hope is one of the most charming of all the stations in this collection.

Victorian flair is the key word here. The station's features include its small, irregularly-shaped frame structure, colored windowpanes and Norman tower.

Quaint New Hope station has been moved twice in recent years and is presently at its original site. It was built in 1889 and was formerly served by the New Hope Branch of the Reading Company.

Purchased from the Reading in the 1960's by the New Hope & Ivyland, a common carrier railroad, the station at New Hope has become a famous local landmark. Now restored, it is home base for the steam train that delights young and old as it makes its 17-mile trip across historic Solebury and Buckingham Townships.

WYCOMBE, PENNSYLVANIA

On June 19, 1891, plans for a depot were
completed and construction was soon
started. Until that time a passenger car
was used as a combination ticket and
freight office. A permanent installation
was needed to accommodate the busy
community, then known as Walton
Station, on the New Hope Branch of The
Reading Company.

CHATSWORTH, NEW JERSEY

Located in the heart of the Pine Barrens in south-central New Jersey, it has no passenger service today, but is used for the area's well-known crops of cranberries and blueberries, and lumber.

FANWOOD-SCOTCH PLAINS, NEW JERSEY

The westbound station pictured here was built about 1868. This depot was part of the Central Railroad of New Jersey. It has been restored and is maintained by the local Junior Chamber of Commerce.

The overpass is of steel construction with timber. It was built in 1942 and remained an open walkway until a roof was added in 1948.

Ranulph Bye

77

Ranulph Bye

GREAT MEADOWS, NEW JERSEY

This station was completed in 1883 at an approximate cost of $3,000. It was used by the Federal Express between Boston and Washington until 1917, although it is doubtful that trains ever stopped. It was then used by The Lehigh and Hudson River Railroad Company which is now gone. Passenger service was discontinued in 1939.

Collection of John A. Meyer, Jr., Coach Inn, Ft. Washington, Pa.

DEMAREST, NEW JERSEY

The steeple on this depot distinguishes
it from the average commuter station.
Built in 1869 of stone, it was once part
of the Erie Railroad system, and is still
in existence though out of service.

Ranulph Bye

ELIZABETH, NEW JERSEY

The Elizabeth station is a stop on Penn Central's New York-Washington main line, as well as a commuter station on the Central Railroad's route to points along the New Jersey shore.

The eastbound building shown here was built between 1891 and 1892. The lower portion is quarry-faced stone, the upper is yellow glazed brick. The clock at the top of the 76-foot tower has not succumbed to automation; it has to be wound by hand once a week.

HACKENSACK, NEW JERSEY

The station at Anderson Street, completed about 1869, was originally on the New Jersey & New York Railroad, later the Erie Railroad. It is 14½ miles from Jersey City and still in service.

In order to complete more fully the composition, the Victorian house to the right of the station was added and the signal tower on the extreme right moved.

HAMMONTON, NEW JERSEY

Sixty miles of railroad track were completed by the Camden & Atlantic Railroad in 1854. The train's route originated at Camden (Cooper's Ferry), with passenger pick-ups at Hammonton and Egg Harbor City. It terminated at Atlantic City.

The original depot was only a short distance from the present Bellevue Avenue location, established in 1858. Hammonton station later became part of the Pennsylvania-Reading Seashore Lines.

HILLSDALE, NEW JERSEY

Originally served by the New Jersey &
New York Railroad and later by the Erie,
the station at Hillsdale is of frame
construction with a slate roof. It was
built in 1869. Hillsdale is about 22 miles
north of Jersey City.

HOBOKEN TERMINAL
HOBOKEN, NEW JERSEY
Kenneth Murchison, architect
Lincoln Bush, engineer

This terminal, built by the Lackawanna Railroad (Delaware, Lackawanna and Western) in 1907, although modest in comparison to New York's Grand Central Station and the now demolished Pennsylvania Station, also in New York, is a monument in its own right. First owned by the Lackawanna, after a merger, the terminal was operated by the Erie-Lackawanna Railroad; today Conrail manages the landmark which has funneled untold numbers of commuters into ferries, tubes and trains for three-quarters of a century. The river-front side stretches seven hundred and fifty feet, and the combined train and ferry terminal is scheduled for rehabilitation with Public Works money. The trainsheds, designed by the engineer and known as Bush sheds, were an innovation for their day. They rest on column-and-girder framing with narrow smoke slots.

Every day one hundred and thirty-two trains arrive and depart, a busy schedule for any terminal. When the ferries stopped operating in October, 1967, the busses took over.

Hopewell, N.J.
Ranulph Bye

HOPEWELL, NEW JERSEY

The two-story brick building at Hopewell is an excellent example of the mansardic era, also known as the "General Grant" style. It was built in 1882 for the Delaware & Bound Brook Railroad.

The railroad line, opened in May, 1876, was one of the carriers built for excursionists from New York (via the Central Railroad of New Jersey) to the Philadelphia Centennial. The Philadelphia & Reading acquired the original road in 1879.

The colorful and fascinating interior of the ticket office is shown at right. Today, the future of this station is uncertain and in a bad state of disrepair.

JERSEY CITY, NEW JERSEY

Communipaw Terminal at Jersey City is the third and final, built between 1913-15, out of deference to modernization and the need for expansion. Like its predecessors, it was both a train and ferry facility, a major commuter station to Manhattan.

The first structure was built in 1864, the second in 1890. Both outlived their ability to accommodate more tracks, bigger trains.

Commuters often had the company of celebrities and "big name" bands, because of available connections to and from the resort areas of New Jersey and Pennsylvania.

A detail of its clock tower is shown at right.

Collection of John A. Meyer, Jr., Coach Inn, Ft. Washington, Pa.

Ranulph Bye

LAMBERTVILLE, NEW JERSEY

The original building, a frame structure, was replaced by the present station in 1871. The depot is noted for its massive size, large dormer windows and unusual cupola. Until 1906 it housed the general offices of the superintendent of the Belvedere-Delaware Railroad.

After the Civil War, Lambertville station was an important machine and repair shop for the Pennsylvania Railroad. [The old Belvedere-Delaware was purchased by the Pennsy in 1971].

The station is located on a narrow belt of land between the Delaware River and the Raritan Canal. In 1982 the station was beautifully remodeled into an attractive restaurant.

Rudolph Bye

LYNDHURST, NEW JERSEY

On the Delaware, Lackawanna & Western
Railroad, the depot was built on high
foundations in order to match the height
of the tract.

The westbound depot had the station
area level with the track; living quarters
were below.

The station was completed in 1883,
gone in 1972.

MANVILLE-FINDERNE, NEW JERSEY

Built in 1878, the two-story frame depot
at Manville-Finderne was a Central Railroad
of New Jersey stop between Plainfield
and Somerville. The road was operative
in 1841, and had extended tracks as far
as Phillipsburg by 1852. The depot was
torn down in the spring of 1972.

MILFORD, NEW JERSEY

The station is now a shop and the tracks
are gone. It is regrettable because it is
located on one of the most scenic rail
lines to be found anywhere. Originating at
Trenton and following the upstream
course of the Delaware River for over 60
miles, the Belvedere-Delaware then
connected with the Lackawanna Railroad.
    Completed in the 1880's, the station is
of half stone, half timber construction.

94

Ranulph Bye

MT. HOLLY, NEW JERSEY

It used to be a busy place, only 20 miles from Philadelphia, including the ferry distance across the Delaware River. The Philadelphia & Long Branch Railroad once had a stop there, later the Pennsylvania line. Now restored.

Ranulph Bye

PENNINGTON, NEW JERSEY

This station is almost identical in design to the one at Hopewell, except that Pennington is a stone structure, not brick.

Completed in 1882, the station was built on a railroad line opened in May, 1876. It was originally served by the Delaware & Bound Brook Railroad and later leased by the Reading.

The Pennington depot is not in service, but its living quarters on the second floor were once used by a Reading Company agent and his family.

SKILLMAN, NEW JERSEY

Completed in 1879, the station is similar
to the one at Weston-Manville. This view
looking north shows the platform and
bay window of the agent's office as of
October, 1964, two years before the
station was razed.

TENAFLY, NEW JERSEY

The painting to the right shows the most notable feature of the Tenafly station— the distinctive green cupola topped by a hand-wrought weathervane.

Many similar stations outside the cities of New York, Boston and Philadelphia were ornately designed. This was indicative of the affluent communities in which they were located.

Tenafly station was built in 1880 by the Northern Railroad of New Jersey; it was acquired by the town of Tenafly in 1963.

WESTON-MANVILLE, NEW JERSEY

Weston-Manville station was built in 1882
by the Philadelphia-Reading Railroad.
The original line, the Delaware & Bound
Brook, had begun service on the track in
May, 1876. It was a 27-mile line from
Bound Brook through Weston-Manville,
Hopewell and Pennington to West
Trenton, formerly Trenton Junction.

Photo by Pennsylvania Historical and Museum Commission, Harrisburg, Pennsylvania

BRONX, NEW YORK

Located at 174th Street and Hoe Avenue, the elevated station illustrated has all the manifestations of the Victorian era . . . colorful glass, wood and iron ornamentation.

The concept of the elevated railway was a marvel of its time and a tremendous engineering feat. It provided the maximum utilization of space, while allowing for pedestrian and auto traffic below, a rapid, mass transit system above.

FORT EDWARD, NEW YORK

55 miles north of Troy, the station was
built for the Delaware & Hudson after
1900.
   On the Saratoga Division of the
Delaware & Hudson. During the time the
D&H ran passenger trains the Laurentian
stopped there during the day and the
Montrealer at night, (Both in both
directions).
   The D&H is now part of Guilford
Industries, the holding company for the
new trunk line composed of Maine
Central, Boston & Maine and D&H.

102

KINGSTON, NEW YORK

This lovely old town is 90 miles northwest of New York City. The former station, torn down in 1964, was probably laid out as a combination depot-hotel complete with dining room. Completed in the late 1860's, it was on the defunct New York, Ontario & Western Railroad.

PEEKSKILL, NEW YORK

Built in 1896 for the New York Central
Railroad, the station at Peekskill is gone,
another victim of time.
　During the railroad era the downtown
hotel across the street from the station
was as much a part of the scene as the
depot itself.

SPARKILL, NEW YORK

In 1844 the first woodburning train began
operating; in 1959 the first train departed
Sparkill to Jersey City.

The station illustrated was built in
1878; once served by the Northern
Railroad of New Jersey, later by the
Erie-Lackawanna.

The town of Sparkill acquired the depot
in the mid-1960's but had it razed in 1972.

WURTSBORO, NEW YORK

Located 26 miles northeast of Port Jervis
on the Port Jervis & Kingston Division,
the one-story frame building at Wurtsboro
is part of the New York, Ontario &
Western Railroad which was abandoned
about 1957.

CANAAN, CONNECTICUT

At one time Canaan was the busy junction and crossing of the New York, New Haven & Hartford and the Central New England Railroads. The station itself dates back to 1872. In the early 1900's, 16 trains of the New Haven and 20 trains of the Central New England stopped here.

The destination of the New Haven line was the Berkshires; the Central New England ran from Hartford to Poughkeepsie.

COS COB, CONNECTICUT

A simple frame structure, still in service, it is representative of many of the stations along the main line of the New Haven Railroad between New York and Boston. It was built sometime between 1880 and 1910, and is located near the Connecticut-New York State boundary.

mulph Bye

OLD SAYBROOK, CONNECTICUT

This large frame structure, built in 1873,
is typical of the frame buildings of the
New Haven Railroad.

The depot is still in use, with a ticket
agent on duty to serve travelers to New
York, 96 miles away.

STAMFORD, CONNECTICUT

The signal tower at Stamford is typical of the many signal towers along the main line of the New Haven Railroad.

Ranulph Bye

111

THOMASTON, CONNECTICUT

This architectural detail of the Thomaston
station shows the overhanging roof and
intricately designed brackets. The station
is still extant.

WATERBURY, CONNECTICUT

The construction date for the Waterbury station was in 1909. With its very high clock tower it is a near replica of the Palazzo Vecchio in Florence, Italy.

The station is now used as the offices of a newspaper since discontinuance of service by the New Haven.

Ranulph Bye

PEACEDALE, RHODE ISLAND

The Narraganset Pier Railroad, founded in 1872, served this station.

Note the interesting bracket treatment over the door and bay windows of the two-story structure. Both the railroad and the depot were recently purchased by a dentist who is also a railroad buff, and he and his family live on the second floor of the station. His plans are to begin excursion trips three days a week; the train will run between Peacedale and Narraganset Pier.

anolph Bye

BUZZARDS BAY, MASSACHUSETTS

The station at Buzzards Bay, built in 1913, was part of the New Haven Railroad.

The white depot, with its brick and stucco construction, tile roof and floor, evokes a definite Spanish flavor. Another noteworthy feature, indicative of the engineering skill of the time, is the drawbridge behind the station which crosses the Cape Cod Canal.

 mulph Bye

CHATHAM, MASSACHUSETTS

The station was completed in 1887.
Service to Chatham was started by the
Chatham Railroad, which became part of
the Old Colony Railroad, later a division
of the New Haven System.

The well-preserved building with its
finely proportioned octagonal tower and
roof of "feather-tipped" shingles is now
a railroad museum, having been restored
by the town of Chatham.

WHITMAN, MASSACHUSETTS

The New York, New Haven & Hartford
Railroad once served this depot. Whitman
is located 21 miles from South Station,
Boston. The station was destroyed by
fire in the summer of 1972.

MIDDLEBURY, VERMONT

This station is on the defunct Rutland Railway, over which trains such as the Green Mountain Flyer once sped between New York and Montreal.

Contracts disposing of stations to private businesses usually contain an extra clause which stipulates that the buyer must move the building away from the railroad's right-of-way. The station, now an auto parts supply store, is on the same site, since the clause was omitted in the purchase agreement.

Ranulph Bye

CRAWFORD NOTCH, NEW HAMPSHIRE

Located in the heart of the White
Mountains, the Crawford Notch station is
85 miles northwest of Portland, Maine.
Now closed, this station was once served
by the Maine Central Railroad.

The Crawford House, which dates back
to the 1870's, can be seen in the
background; it is still a flourishing hotel.

Collection of John A. Myer, Jr., Fort Washington, Pennsylvania

NORTH CONWAY, NEW HAMPSHIRE

Located at the southern entrance to the White Mountains region, North Conway is 137 miles north of Boston.

This imposing station was designed by the well-known Boston architect, Nathaniel J. Bradlee and completed in 1872, and it was served by the Boston & Maine Railroad. It was designed to conform with the opulent resort hotels built during the latter half of the 19th century. It is, today, a prototype of the railroad station of its time, and is to be restored and used as the depot for a steam railroad, a tourist attraction.

125

MURPHYSBORO, ILLINOIS

This station was built for the Gulf, Mobile
& Ohio R.R. in 1888, formerly Mobile &
Ohio. The depot is now out of service and
in disrepair.

VIENNA JUNCTION SIGNAL TOWER

Chicago & Eastern/Illinois R.R.